2018 SQA Specimen and Past Papers with Answers

Higher
BUSINESS MANAGEMENT

2016, 2017 & 2018 Exams
and 2018 Specimen Question Paper

HODDER
GIBSON
AN HACHETTE UK COMPANY

This book contains the official SQA 2016, 2017 and 2018 Exams, and the 2018 Specimen Question Paper for Higher Business Management, with associated SQA-approved answers modified from the official marking instructions that accompany the paper.

In addition the book contains study skills advice. This advice has been specially commissioned by Hodder Gibson, and has been written by experienced senior teachers and examiners in line with the Higher syllabus and assessment outlines. This is not SQA material but has been devised to provide further guidance for Higher examinations.

Hodder Gibson is grateful to the copyright holders, as credited on the final page of the Answer section, for permission to use their material. Every effort has been made to trace the copyright holders and to obtain their permission for the use of copyright material. Hodder Gibson will be happy to receive information allowing us to rectify any error or omission in future editions.

The information about BT Group plc ("BT"), contained in the exam question on pages 2-4 of the 2018 exam paper, is based on historic information made available by BT and may no longer be accurate. For current information about BT, please visit www.btplc.com.

Hachette UK's policy is to use papers that are natural, renewable and recyclable products and made from wood grown in sustainable forests. The logging and manufacturing processes are expected to conform to the environmental regulations of the country of origin.

Orders: please contact Bookpoint Ltd, 130 Park Drive, Milton Park, Abingdon, Oxon OX14 4SE. Telephone: (44) 01235 827827. Fax: (44) 01235 400454. Lines are open 9.00–5.00, Monday to Saturday, with a 24-hour message answering service. Visit our website at www.hoddereducation.co.uk. Hodder Gibson can also be contacted directly at hoddergibson@hodder.co.uk

This collection first published in 2018 by
Hodder Gibson, an imprint of Hodder Education,
An Hachette UK Company
211 St Vincent Street
Glasgow G2 5QY

Typeset by Aptara, Inc.

Printed in the UK.

A catalogue record for this title is available from the British Library.

ISBN: 978-1-5104-5701-0

2 1

2019 2018

Introduction

Higher Business Management

This book of SQA past papers contains the question papers used in the 2016, 2017 and 2018 exams (with the answers at the back of the book). A specimen question paper reflecting the requirements, content and duration of the revised exam in 2019 is also included. All of the question papers included in the book provide excellent, representative practice for the final exams.

Using the past papers as part of your revision will help you to develop the vital skills and techniques needed for the exam, and will help you to identify any knowledge gaps you may have.

It is always a very good idea to refer to SQA's website for the most up-to-date course specification documents. Further details can be found in the Higher Business Management section on the SQA website: www.sqa.org.uk/sqa/47919.html

The exams

Higher Business Management is assessed in two ways: through an Assignment (worth 30 marks, and 25% of your final grade) and a Question Paper (the Exam). The Exam is formed of two sections, which together are work 90 marks – 75% of your final grade.

From 2019, the exam will last 2 hours 45 minutes. This is 30 minutes longer than the exams in previous years.

This book contains official past papers from 2016, 2017 and 2018. These exams were designed to be taken in 2 hours 15 minutes. You should try to stick to this timing when using these papers for practice.

From 2019, the question paper will be extended by 20 marks. The duration of the exam will increase by 30 minutes, to 2 hours 45 minutes. The specimen question paper included in the book reflects the duration of the updated exam. So, don't forget that you have 2 hours 45 minutes when you practise using this specimen paper.

It is important for you to be aware that in all of the papers (2016, 2017, 2018 and the specimen question paper) **there is no choice of questions**. The structure of the examination is outlined below.

Section one

This is based on a case study of approximately 700 words and it will include additional information in the form of exhibits (appendices). The exhibits could include financial information, graphs or charts, pictorial information, timelines, etc.

This will be followed by a total of 30 marks' worth of questions. Most of the questions will relate to information contained in the case study and exhibits, and may make reference to that information. It is important that your answers to the questions relate back to the information in the case study and exhibits. There will be a maximum of around eight questions which may be split into parts. The questions can be drawn from any area of the course and will use a variety of different command words. The aim of this section of the paper is to test breadth of knowledge from any part of the course.

Section two

This section of the examination paper is made up of four questions worth 15 marks each. The 15 marks will be split into a maximum of three parts in most cases, although you may see some questions split into just two parts. The aim of this section of the paper is to test depth of knowledge and each 15-mark question will focus on one topic area of the course. The questions can be drawn from any area of the course and will use a variety of different command words.

The main topic areas of the course, which you should already know, that are available to test are:

1. *Understanding business*
2. *People*
3. *Finance*
4. *Marketing*
5. *Operations*

Additionally, *Technology* is a theme that is covered across all of these topic areas so you should be prepared to apply this knowledge at any point in the exam. Whilst areas 2, 3, 4 and 5 are fairly equally weighted, area 1 is large in comparison so it is fair to expect to be asked statistically more questions from this area of the course.

Answering questions in Higher Business Management

Read the question carefully

It is often easy to assume you know what you are being asked in a question by picking out a few keywords. You will be in a high-pressure situation whether you think you are or not, and it's easy to try and get through the paper quickly. Take the time you need to read the question carefully. It is essential that you answer the question being asked in order to maximise the number of marks that you can achieve. No question is deliberately worded to catch you out, or be a test of English, but you do need to understand how and why command words are used.

For example, "Describe the role of managers in staff appraisals" caused problems for many candidates as they either described the role of the manager or staff appraisals. This did not answer the question and so they could not be given marks. The role of manager had to be *related* to staff appraisals in order to answer the question fully and correctly.

Answering the command words

Each question in Higher Business Management has a command word to help you understand what is needed in your response. Some of the most common command words used are listed below with an explanation of what is required in your response. This list is not exhaustive and other command words could be used. Typically, in the Higher Business Management examination papers, "describe" is the most commonly used command, while the command which causes candidates the most problems (possibly because it demands more knowledge and application of that knowledge) is "explain".

Commonly used command words

Describe requires a more detailed answer, giving the main features. It must be a description of something. Additional marks may be available if you give examples in, or further depth to, your description. These are sometimes referred to as development points.

For example, *"A loan from a bank which is repaid over time in equal instalments with interest"*.

Justify will ask you to give reasons why a particular course of action would be used by a business. Here you would be asked to give the benefits that the course of action would bring to the business.

Discuss normally requires you to give advantages and disadvantages, or both sides of an argument. It is not always necessary to give both sides of the debate to be awarded full marks, provided that your points are fully developed.

For example, "Discuss the use of bank loans for a business".

Answers could include: *"Allows the business to spread repayments over a longer period of time, which will help with cash flow"* and *"The business will have to pay interest on the money borrowed"*.

Distinguish requires you to list the differences between two things. It is important to understand that you only get **one mark** for each distinguishing point.

For example, "Distinguish between a bank loan and a mortgage".

To answer this question you need to say what the differences are: *"A bank loan is normally for a short period such as 5 years, whereas a mortgage is for a much longer period such as 30 years"*. Note that this discussion point would be worth only one mark.

Compare is similar in some ways to distinguish, but also allows you to write what is similar as well as what the differences are.

For example, "Compare a bank loan and a mortgage".

Answers could include the distinguishing point above, but also similarities such as *"Both are repaid with added interest"*.

Explain requires a more detailed answer. Essentially it can be thought of as a description plus an explanation of why something is the way it is.

For example, "Explain the disadvantages of a bank loan for a business".

Your answer would need to be developed, such as: *"Added interest would need to be repaid, which would adversely affect the costs to the business"*. Added interest on its own would not gain a mark as it does not actually explain why the bank loan is a disadvantage for the business.

Good luck!

Remember that the rewards for passing Higher Business Management are well worth it! Your pass will help you get the future you want for yourself. In the exam, be confident in your own ability. If you're not sure how to answer a question, trust your instincts and just give it a go anyway – keep calm and don't panic! GOOD LUCK!

Study Skills – what you need to know to pass exams!

General exam revision: 20 top tips

When preparing for exams, it is easy to feel unsure of where to start or how to revise. This guide to general exam revision provides a good starting place, and, as these are very general tips, they can be applied to all your exams.

1. Start revising in good time.

Don't leave revision until the last minute – this will make you panic and it will be difficult to learn. Make a revision timetable that counts down the weeks to go.

2. Work to a study plan.

Set up sessions of work spread through the weeks ahead. Make sure each session has a focus and a clear purpose. What will you study, when and why? Be realistic about what you can achieve in each session, and don't be afraid to adjust your plans as needed.

3. Make sure you know exactly when your exams are.

Get your exam dates from the SQA website and use the timetable builder tool to create your own exam schedule. You will also get a personalised timetable from your school, but this might not be until close to the exam period.

4. Make sure that you know the topics that make up each course.

Studying is easier if material is in manageable chunks – why not use the SQA topic headings or create your own from your class notes? Ask your teacher for help on this if you are not sure.

5. Break the chunks up into even smaller bits.

The small chunks should be easier to cope with. Remember that they fit together to make larger ideas. Even the process of chunking down will help!

6. Ask yourself these key questions for each course:

- Are all topics compulsory or are there choices?
- Which topics seem to come up time and time again?
- Which topics are your strongest and which are your weakest?

Use your answers to these questions to work out how much time you will need to spend revising each topic.

7. Make sure you know what to expect in the exam.

The subject-specific introduction to this book will help with this. Make sure you can answer these questions:

- How is the paper structured?
- How much time is there for each part of the exam?
- What types of question are involved? These will vary depending on the subject so read the subject-specific section carefully.

8. Past papers are a vital revision tool!

Use past papers to support your revision wherever possible. This book contains the answers and mark schemes too – refer to these carefully when checking your work. Using the mark scheme is useful; even if you don't manage to get all the marks available first time when you first practise, it helps you identify how to extend and develop your answers to get more marks next time – and of course, in the real exam.

9. Use study methods that work well for you.

People study and learn in different ways. Reading and looking at diagrams suits some students. Others prefer to listen and hear material – what about reading out loud or getting a friend or family member to do this for you? You could also record and play back material.

10. There are three tried and tested ways to make material stick in your long-term memory:

- Practising – e.g. rehearsal, repeating
- Organising – e.g. making drawings, lists, diagrams, tables, memory aids
- Elaborating – e.g. incorporating the material into a story or an imagined journey

11. Learn actively.

Most people prefer to learn actively – for example, making notes, highlighting, redrawing and redrafting, making up memory aids, or writing past paper answers. A good way to stay engaged and inspired is to mix and match these methods – find the combination that best suits you. This is likely to vary depending on the topic or subject.

12. Be an expert.

Be sure to have a few areas in which you feel you are an expert. This often works because at least some of them will come up, which can boost confidence.

13. Try some visual methods.

Use symbols, diagrams, charts, flashcards, post-it notes etc. Don't forget – the brain takes in chunked images more easily than loads of text.

14. Remember – practice makes perfect.

Work on difficult areas again and again. Look and read – then test yourself. You cannot do this too much.

15. Try past papers against the clock.

Practise writing answers in a set time. This is a good habit from the start but is especially important when you get closer to exam time.

16. Collaborate with friends.

Test each other and talk about the material – this can really help. Two brains are better than one! It is amazing how talking about a problem can help you solve it.

17. Know your weaknesses.

Ask your teacher for help to identify what you don't know. Try to do this as early as possible. If you are having trouble, it is probably with a difficult topic, so your teacher will already be aware of this – most students will find it tough.

18. Have your materials organised and ready.

Know what is needed for each exam:

- Do you need a calculator or a ruler?
- Should you have pencils as well as pens?
- Will you need water or paper tissues?

19. Make full use of school resources.

Find out what support is on offer:

- Are there study classes available?
- When is the library open?
- When is the best time to ask for extra help?
- Can you borrow textbooks, study guides, past papers, etc.?
- Is school open for Easter revision?

20. Keep fit and healthy!

Try to stick to a routine as much as possible, including with sleep. If you are tired, sluggish or dehydrated, it is difficult to see how concentration is even possible. Combine study with relaxation, drink plenty of water, eat sensibly, and get fresh air and exercise – all these things will help more than you could imagine. Good luck!

HIGHER

2016

National
Qualifications
2016

X710/76/11

Business Management

FRIDAY, 27 MAY
9:00 AM — 11:15 AM

Total marks — 70

SECTION 1 — 30 marks

Attempt ALL questions.

SECTION 2 — 40 marks

Attempt ALL questions.

It is recommended that you spend 15 minutes reading over the information provided in **SECTION 1** before responding to the questions.

Write your answers clearly in the answer booklet provided. In the answer booklet, you must clearly identify the question number you are attempting.

Use **blue** or **black** ink.

Before leaving the examination room you must give your answer booklet to the Invigilator; if you do not, you may lose all the marks for this paper.

SECTION 1 — 30 marks

Read ALL the following information and attempt ALL the questions that follow.

Mackie's of Scotland: Greener the better

Luxury ice cream producer Mackie's of Scotland is not shy about promoting its green aspirations. The company states that it wants to become a global brand, and in terms of sustainability, the greenest company in Britain.

Ice cream, crisps and chocolate

Mackie's runs its operations from a 1,600 acre dairy farm in Aberdeenshire where raw materials are sourced from neighbouring farms. The company has a 7% share of the total UK ice cream market with sales of over 10 million litres every year.

In 2004 Mackie's launched "Mackice" by selling ice cubes made from locally sourced spring water. In 2009 Mackie's branched out into crisps when it formed a joint venture with Perthshire-based potato processor Taypack. It now exports to markets in over 20 countries and has expanded into the chocolate confectionery market.

Driven by the desire for absolute customer satisfaction, Mackie's has invested in computer controlled mass-production machinery so that 6,000 litres of ice cream per hour can be produced in order to cope with increasing demand. Products go through rigorous quality assurance and control measures before goods are released for distribution to retailers. There is also a highly trained taste panel which benchmarks new products with competitors.

Investment in renewable energy

One of Mackie's most ambitious goals incorporates the entire site: to become 100% self-sufficient in renewable energy. This fits with the Scottish Government's target of generating the equivalent of 100% of Scotland's gross national electricity consumption from renewable sources by 2020.

Mackie's installed its first 50 kW wind turbine in 1983 which produced enough energy to heat a piggery. The technology applied to wind farms has improved drastically in the intervening years and, via the three modern turbines currently on site, Mackie's has an installed renewable energy capacity of 2·5 MW.

Mackie's estimates that since the installation of the turbines, it has saved approximately 3,480 tonnes of carbon emissions that would otherwise have been produced by the company's day-to-day operations.

Mackie's Marketing Director, Karin Hayhow, said: "The wind turbines are incredibly efficient and have performed much better than expected, largely due to the good location we occupy and the fact that Scotland is the windiest country in Europe".

"However we also have a lot of other exciting projects, such as having on-site injection moulders to make our own tubs." This required an investment of over £1 million and reduced emissions from not having to import packaging from Sweden.

As well as utilising wind to produce energy, Mackie's is also harnessing solar power. In February 2012 150 kW of solar panels were installed on the site. "Through this, we are saving almost £500,000 per year on our electricity bills, and with electricity prices increasing, our savings are only set to rise. This enables us to invest in more efficient machinery and processes that, in turn, help to keep the cost of production down."

Looking to the future

Mackie's is in no way finished with its energy efficiency campaign and has a series of projects that it is looking to implement in the near future:

- Construct a fourth wind turbine.
- Build a 1·5 MW solar farm to increase renewable capacity.
- Invest in electric vehicles on the farm for the use of staff.

Mackie's Finance Director, Gerry Stephens, said: "For any business, managing the bottom line is essential, and cutting energy costs as well as reducing carbon emissions should always be included in any robust business plan."

[Turn over

Further Information

Exhibit 1

Overview of Mackie's renewable and sustainability

Solar Energy	The company has over 700 solar panels which generate electricity to power various parts of the farm and the milking robots.
Zero Waste Water	Waste water is pumped back over the land. The cows also drink the clean waste water.
Natural Fertiliser	The slurry from the cows is used as natural fertiliser, reducing the amount of commercial fertiliser which is bought.
Harnessing Wind	Mackie's commercial turbine was installed in 2005 with a further investment of £1·7 million to add two more in 2007. These two new turbines have more than trebled the electricity generated, saving the company £280,000 a year in electricity bills. Mackie's makes a surplus of energy which is sold to the company Good Energy.
Recycling Packaging	Mackie's recycles cardboard, plastic, wood, batteries and metal.

Adapted from: mackies.co.uk; thescottishfarmer.co.uk

Exhibit 2

Additional information on marketing activities

2002	2004	2010	2012	2013
Official ice cream sponsor of the World Cup in South Korea.	Launched low fat chocolate iced dessert suitable for diabetics.	Sponsor of the Macrobert JustGiving appeal to support deprived families.	New website to promote news, competitions and get valuable customer feedback.	Launched a television advert to further promote its ice cream.

Adapted from: mackies.co.uk

Exhibit 3

Extract from Mackie's social media site informing customers of special offers

Mackie's Ice Cream
12 September

Great offer at Tesco Scottish stores only . . . 1 litre Traditional, Honeycomb, Strawberry, Chocolate, Chocolate Mint and Raspberry Ripple — SAVE £1. Offer ends 15th September. Happy shopping!

Like · Comment · Share   200 Shares

118 people like this

[Turn over

Exhibit 4

Summary of financial performance

	2011 £	2012 £	2013 £
Revenue (Sales)	11,629,244	11,509,252	10,284,432
Gross Profit	5,079,814	4,913,867	4,322,633
Profit for year (Net Profit)	255,682	197,079	546,801

Adapted from: companieshouse.gov.uk

MARKS

The following questions are based on ALL the information provided and on knowledge and understanding you have gained whilst studying the course.

1. (a) (i) Describe **2** suitable pricing strategies for Mackie's luxury ice cream produce. Unit 2

4

(ii) Discuss the "out of the pipeline" methods of promotion identified in the case study. Unit 2

4

(b) Explain, using examples from the case study, the benefits to Mackie's of having a diverse product portfolio. Unit 2

4

(c) Describe the reasons why Mackie's heavily invested in renewable energy methods. Unit 2

3

(d) Compare the method of production used by Mackie's with job production.

4

(e) Discuss the methods of ensuring quality identified in the case study. Unit 2

5

(f) (i) Describe the ratios which could be calculated from the financial information in **Exhibit 4**.

3

(ii) Using **Exhibit 4**, explain the trends in Mackie's profits.

3

[Turn over for next question

MARKS

SECTION 2 — 40 marks

Attempt ALL questions

2. (a) ~~Describe the methods which may be used to motivate employees.~~   4

   (b) Explain the benefits of an appraisal system. *Unit 2*   4

   (c) Describe the benefits of workforce planning. *Unit 2*   2

3. (a) Explain the advantages of internal (organic) growth. *Unit 1*   4

   (b) ~~Discuss the use of geographical grouping.~~   3

   (c) Describe the advantages of being a social enterprise. *Unit 1*   3

4. (a) (i) Describe the impact of competition policy on an organisation.   2

       (ii) Other than competition, explain the impact of external factors on an organisation. *Unit 1*   5

   (b) Distinguish between a tactical decision and an operational decision. *Unit 1*   3

5. (a) Justify the use of spreadsheets within the finance department.   4

   (b) Other than spreadsheets, describe how modern technology can be used by the finance department.   6

[END OF QUESTION PAPER]

HIGHER

2017

National Qualifications 2017

X710/76/11   **Business Management**

TUESDAY, 16 MAY

9:00 AM — 11:15 AM

Total marks — 70

SECTION 1 — 30 marks

Attempt ALL questions

SECTION 2 — 40 marks

Attempt ALL questions

It is recommended that you spend 15 minutes reading over the information provided in **SECTION 1** before responding to the questions.

Write your answers clearly in the answer booklet provided. In the answer booklet, you must clearly identify the question number you are attempting.

Use **blue** or **black** ink.

Before leaving the examination room you must give your answer booklet to the Invigilator; if you do not, you may lose all the marks for this paper.

Section 1 of this Question Paper replaces the original SQA Past Paper 2017, which cannot be reproduced for copyright reasons. As such, it should be stressed that it is not an official SQA-verified section, although every care has been taken by the Publishers to ensure that it offers appropriate practice material for Higher Business Management.

SECTION 1 — 30 marks

Read ALL the following information and attempt ALL the questions that follow.

The following information has been taken from the Mary's Meals website.

Mary's Meals

Mary's Meals is a charity that works to support a school feeding programme for over 920,000 children across the world. It all started in 1992 when two brothers, Magnus and Fergus MacFarlane-Barrow, were watching the television news coverage of the Bosnian conflict. They started an appeal for food and blankets and filled a Jeep and drove to Bosnia. When they returned and went back to work, they discovered that donations were still arriving. Magnus gave up his job for a year and kept making trips to Bosnia with donations. The donations didn't stop and Magnus set up a charity, Scottish International Relief, which expanded its work into Romania, Liberia and Croatia. By 2002, the charity was  supporting a famine relief project in Malawi. As Magnus helped support the children of a mother who was dying of AIDS, the inspiration for Mary's Meals was born: to provide chronically hungry children with one meal every school day. This helps to encourage children to gain education and lift them out of poverty. By 2014, the charity now known as Mary's Meals was providing meals to children in Africa, Asia, the Caribbean, Eastern Europe and South America.

A simple solution to world hunger

For many children, Mary's Meals may be the only meal they will have in a day. In Malawi, it costs £8.20 to provide Mary's Meals to one child for a whole school year and an average of £12.20 per child per year globally. The meals are made using locally produced food wherever possible. This respects local culture and tastes and avoids transport costs.

The charity also works in partnership with local communities wherever possible. In Malawi, over 60,000 volunteers cook and serve over 600,000 meals every school day.

Mary's Meals aims to spend at least 93p of every £1 that is donated to carry out charitable work. It does this by making extensive use of volunteers and by monitoring and controlling costs to keep them as low as possible.

It works with other partner organisations and supports other charitable work. (See Exhibit 1 and Exhibit 3 for more information.)

Ethical and morally responsible business practice

Mary's Meals can be seen to be an ethical business model. It exists to provide a service to people using resources that have been donated by other people. The Mary's Meals vision is that every child receives one daily meal in their place of education, and that all those who have more than they need share with those who lack even the most basic things.

The mission of the charity is to enable people to offer their money, goods, skills, time, or prayer, and through this involvement, providing the most effective help to those suffering the effects of extreme poverty in the world's poorest communities.

Donations

Mary's Meals is dependent on donations of money in order to operate. The Mary's Meals website is available in different languages and you can make a donation online. It is also possible to make a regular donation to the charity from your bank account or donate by phone, by text or by post. Some people may choose to keep a donation box in their home and encourage visitors who come for dinner to make a donation to Mary's Meals.

Counting on support from around the globe, Mary's Meals has fundraising entities and registered charity arms in Austria, Canada, Croatia, France, Germany, Italy, Ireland, the Netherlands, Portugal, Spain, the United Kingdom and the USA. It promotes the fact that a maximum of 7p in every £1 donated is used for corporate governance.

Source: http://www.marysmeals.org.uk

[Turn over

Further Information

Exhibit 1 — Mary's Meals projects and partnership working

Use of celebrities	Celebrities help raise the profile of the work of the charity, eg Hollywood star Gerard Butler recently visited Mary's Meals in Liberia
The backpack project	Over 420,000 donated backpacks have been sent overseas to help children attending school
Saving Grace	A short animation telling the story of 10-year-old Grace
Sponsor a school	Rather than making a donation to the charity, people or groups are encouraged to sponsor an entire school
Stage a screening of Child 31	A film made to raise awareness of the work of Mary's Meals

Exhibit 2 — Key statistics

Mary's Meals Charity

		Unrestricted funds £	Restricted funds £	2013 Total £	2012 Total £
Incoming resources					
Incoming resources from generated funds:					
Voluntary income	2	8,043,912	3,837,541	11,881,453	7,755,910
Activities for generating funds	3	559,809	—	559,809	1,893,901
Investment income		11,801	—	11,801	8,839
Incoming resources from charitable activities		917	—	917	360
Tax reclaimed on Gift Aid		452,315	16,000	468,315	334,666
Total incoming resources		9,068,754	3,853,541	12,922,295	9,993,676

Exhibit 3 — Facts at a glance

- Total number of children receiving a daily meal in school = 894,288
- Average global cost of Mary's Meals per child, per year = £12.20
- Worldwide average cost per meal = 6 pence
- Number of chronically hungry children in the world = 300 million (around 57 million of these children are out of school)
- Number of backpacks sent overseas in 2014 (so far) = 20,872
- Total number of backpacks delivered to date = 402,680
- In addition to school feeding projects, Mary's Meals supports a children's home project in Romania

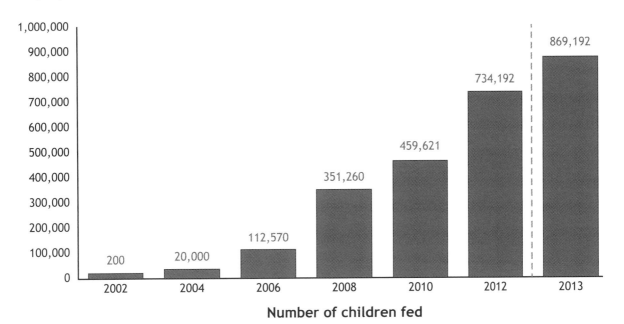

Number of children fed

Exhibit 4 — How money is spent

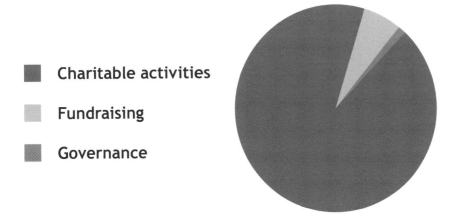

- Charitable activities
- Fundraising
- Governance

[Turn over

MARK

The following questions are based on ALL the information provided and on knowledge and understanding whilst studying the course.

1. (a) Using the case study, compare the objectives of Mary's Meals to a public sector organisation.

    3

    (b) Discuss the potential areas of conflict for Mary's Meals as it mostly operates in overseas countries.

    5

    (c) Describe the promotional strategies used by Mary's Meals to attract donations.

    5

    (d) Explain the importance for Mary's Meals to operate as an ethically responsible business.

    3

    (e) Discuss the market research methods that Mary's Meals could use to gather information from its donors.

    6

    (f) (i) Suggest the reasons for an increase in voluntary income in 2013.

    2

    (ii) Distinguish between two sources of finance which Mary's Meals could use to further expand.

    2

    (g) Describe the impact of internal factors on a charity like Mary's Meals.

    4

MARKS

SECTION 2 — 40 marks

Attempt ALL questions

2. (a) Explain the benefits to an organisation of developing a strong corporate culture.   3

    (b) Describe the effects of widening the span of control of a manager.   5

    (c) Describe examples of conflict that may arise between different groups of stakeholders.   2

3. (a) Discuss the use of benchmarking to ensure quality.   4

    (b) Describe ways an organisation can become environmentally responsible.   3

    (c) Justify the use of job production.   3

4. (a) Explain the benefits of preparing a cash budget.   5

    (b) Describe the impact on an organisation of having poor cash flow.   5

5. (a) Describe the laissez-faire style of leadership.   3

    (b) Describe the impact of current employment legislation on organisations.   4

    (c) Discuss the costs and benefits of work-based qualifications.   3

[END OF QUESTION PAPER]

[BLANK PAGE]

DO NOT WRITE ON THIS PAGE

HIGHER

2018

National Qualifications 2018

X710/76/11

Business Management

FRIDAY, 18 MAY

9:00 AM – 11:15 AM

Total marks — 70

SECTION 1 — 30 marks

Attempt ALL questions

SECTION 2 — 40 marks

Attempt ALL questions

It is recommended that you spend 15 minutes reading over the information provided in **SECTION 1** before responding to the questions.

Write your answers clearly in the answer booklet provided. In the answer booklet you must clearly identify the question number you are attempting.

Use **blue** or **black** ink.

Before leaving the examination room you must give your answer booklet to the Invigilator; if you do not, you may lose all the marks for this paper.

SECTION 1 — 30 marks

Read ALL the following information and attempt ALL the questions that follow.

BT Group PLC

BT is a public limited company, registered on the London Stock Exchange. It was originally a public corporation regulated by the Government; however, the company was privatised in December 1983. BT's shareholders paid the equivalent of £20 billion in today's prices to acquire all the assets of BT.

BT today

BT is a modern communications services company, providing a range of services in the UK and in more than 170 countries. About a quarter of its revenue is earned outside the UK, providing services to multinationals and other large organisations. BT is a global company with around 106,400 employees in 63 countries, of which around 82,800 work in the UK.

In 2015, BT announced a move back into the consumer mobile market by introducing SIM only plans. To accelerate their growth in the highly competitive market of mobile communications, BT acquired the mobile business EE for £12·5 billion. This was subject to clearance from shareholders and the UK Competition and Markets Authority. EE was one of the leading mobile network operators in the UK with 31 million customers and had the largest 4G customer base of any operator in Europe. The aim of the takeover was to combine EE and BT, which would provide customers with innovative and seamless communications services.

Skills and training

BT's management believes that people are the key to the success of the business, therefore getting the best employees is vital. BT has had an apprenticeship scheme in place for over 50 years and recruited around 900 young people last year onto its programme. As well as this, BT has its own training centre, the BT Academy, where employees from all levels within the organisation receive high quality training.

BT and the National Health Service (NHS)

BT has been supplying technology to the UK's NHS for more than 65 years, providing the equipment and technical support required to keep critical services running. Together they created the NHS broadband network which securely connects every GP surgery, hospital and clinic in England. It has also worked with community and mental health organisations, connecting healthcare professionals and transforming the way patient care is delivered.

BT's integrity and ethics

It is important for BT to know who it is doing business with and who is acting on its behalf. BT chooses suppliers using an established set of principles that makes sure both it and the supplier act ethically and responsibly. BT checks that the goods and services it buys are made, delivered, and disposed of in a socially and environmentally responsible way.

BT is committed to minimising its impact on the environment and reducing the carbon intensity of its global business by 80% against 1997 levels by 2020. BT wants to make a positive contribution to society by investing in communities.

Future

BT is one of the largest investors in research and development (R&D) in the UK and the second largest investor in R&D in the telecoms sector in the world. Since 1990, BT has had over 10,000 patents granted. In 2017 BT invested £520 million in R&D.

Gavin Patterson, BT Chief Executive, said: 'I'm really excited about the future and how BT will be right at the heart of shaping it. I'm confident that, with the support of our people, we'll continue to use the power of communications to make a better world.'

Further information

Exhibit 1 — Ratio analysis of BT's financial performance

	2012	2014	2016
Gross Profit Ratio	14%	17%	11%
Profit for the Year Ratio	9%	11%	7%
Current Ratio	0·5:1	0·7:1	0·8:1

Exhibit 2 — BT Retail's product life cycle — 2014

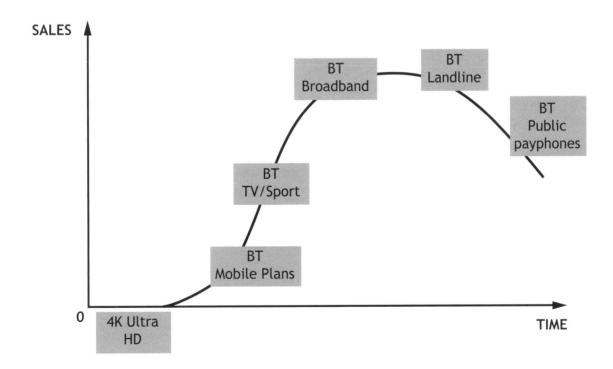

[Turn over

Exhibit 3 — BT's selection process

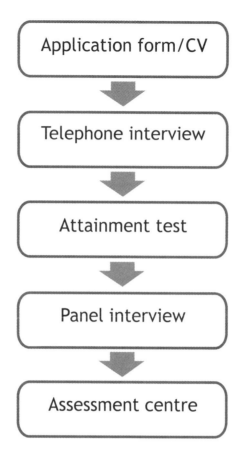

MARKS

The following questions are based on ALL the information provided and on knowledge and understanding you have gained whilst studying the course.

1. (a) Describe the benefits to BT of being a multinational company.

5

   (b) Explain the advantages of BT taking over EE, as detailed in the case study.

4

   (c) With reference to the case study, discuss the methods used by BT to train its staff.

6

   (d) Describe the steps that BT could take to improve its profitability and liquidity ratios.

3

   (e) Explain the impact on profits of the following BT products, as shown in **Exhibit 2**:

   • 4K Ultra HD

   • BT Public payphones.

2

   (f) Discuss the benefits of the selection methods used by BT, as listed in **Exhibit 3**.

6

   (g) Describe potential conflicts between any of the BT stakeholders mentioned in the case study.

4

[Turn over

MARKS

SECTION 2 — 40 marks
Attempt ALL questions

2. (a) Discuss the use of just in time (JIT) production.   5

   (b) Describe the advantages of centralised warehousing.   3

   (c) Justify the expense of investing in robotics for mass production.   2

3. (a) Describe appropriate long-term sources of finance for a large organisation.   4

   (b) Describe the purpose of preparing a Statement of Financial Position.   4

   (c) Justify the use of software such as spreadsheets to record financial information.   2

4. (a) Discuss the methods of market research.   5

   (b) Describe the role of public relations (PR) in an organisation.   3

   (c) Explain the benefits to an organisation of using loss leaders as a pricing tactic.   2

5. (a) Describe the objectives of third sector organisations.   3

   (b) Compare functional grouping with customer grouping.   4

   (c) Explain the impact of environmental factors on an organisation.   3

[END OF QUESTION PAPER]

2018 Specimen Question Paper

Date — Not applicable

Duration — 2 hours 45 minutes

Total marks — 90

SECTION 1 — 30 marks

Attempt ALL questions.

SECTION 2 — 60 marks

Attempt ALL questions.

You may use a calculator.

It is recommended that you spend 15 minutes reading over the information provided in **SECTION 1** before responding to the questions.

Write your answers clearly in the answer booklet provided. In the answer booklet you must clearly identify the question number you are attempting.

Use **blue** or **black** ink.

Before leaving the examination room you must give your answer booklet to the Invigilator; if you do not, you may lose all the marks for this paper.

SECTION 1 — 30 marks

Read ALL the following information and attempt ALL the questions that follow.

Toyota — 'Always a Better Way'

Toyota is one of the world's biggest car companies, selling around 10 million vehicles in 2017. Toyota offers a range of cars for different market segments, including a luxury top-end brand called 'Lexus'. The Toyota website states that it 'has a car for everyone' in its product portfolio. A sample of the portfolio is shown in Exhibit 2.

The global market for cars is expected to continue to increase. Sales are predicted to rise, driven by the global economic recovery, falling fuel prices, low interest rates and higher household disposable income.

Despite its Sports Utility Vehicles (SUVs) being popular in the USA, Toyota may face a fall in demand as the current President wants consumers to purchase American cars.

Production development

Toyota is famous for its lean production techniques such as just-in-time (JIT). Toyota also utilises its staff very effectively. Through quality circles and a suggestion system, team members strive to achieve Toyota's quality management principle of continuous improvement. More than 90,000 employee suggestions are adopted each year, with some individual team members having contributed more than 1,000 suggestions.

While Toyota, like any modern day car manufacturer, has a capital-intensive approach using automated production lines, it places a high importance on its employees and carries out extensive workforce planning. This ensures it has sufficient staff, whilst being aware of the effects of an increasingly mechanised approach on staff numbers. Toyota has launched its own academy to provide learning and skills development covering all aspects of its business.

While an autocratic leadership style is common in manufacturing, Toyota regards all employees as members of the team. All staff are considered important contributors and are given a high level of autonomy.

Leaders in 'green' cars

Toyota's first venture into hybrid technology, which enables cars to run on both fuel and electricity, was the Toyota Prius model.

A hybrid vehicle has two engines, one electric and one conventional fuel, ie petrol or diesel. Unlike an electric car, a hybrid vehicle recharges its own battery on the move when it is being driven by the conventional engine. There is no need to look for a charging point for this type of car or wait for one to become free. It is both fuel efficient and environmentally-friendly since it has significantly low carbon emissions. Venturing into hybrid technology has helped Toyota's customers reduce their carbon footprint.

In order to develop this eco-friendly model further, Toyota rolled out the Prius Plug-in hybrid. The Prius Plug-in can be charged at home or at a charging point for additional power. This can be completed in two hours. The fuel tank is on the left side and a plug-in socket for recharging is on the right side. As a result, the hybrid is more fuel efficient, making it more attractive to the consumer.

Steve Lagreca / Shutterstock.com

Star Safety System

The Toyota Prius Plug-in also excels in terms of safety. The carmaker's Star Safety System ensures that accident avoidance features are in place, such as a system to assist with emergency braking and a camera for reversing.

With Toyota's commitment to continuous improvement, safety, environmental awareness and lean production, it is clear to see why its marketing slogan is 'Always a Better Way'.

Further information

Exhibit 1	
Toyota's SWOT analysis	
Strengths • high worldwide car sales • large product portfolio • an innovator in 'green' car development • extensive workforce planning system • highly recognisable brand	**Weaknesses** • lack of presence in emerging markets, such as China and India • numerous vehicle recalls due to faults
Opportunities • changing customer attitudes towards 'green' cars • falling fuel prices • global economic recovery	**Threats** • competition from General Motors and VW group • rising raw material prices • natural disasters in Japan • fluctuating exchange rates

[Turn over

Exhibit 2 Product portfolio sample 2017		
Model	**Market**	**Price**
Lexus GSF Ed Aldridge / Shutterstock.com	Luxury	£73,375
Toyota Prius Art Konovalov / Shutterstock.com	Eco-friendly	£24,115
Toyota AYGO Dong liu / Shutterstock.com	Economy	£8,995

Exhibit 3 Toyota's ratio analysis		
Ratio	**2016**	**2017**
Current Ratio	1·13:1	1·03:1
Gross Profit Percentage	20·41%	17·62%
Return on Equity Employed	6·27%	4·82%

MARKS

The following questions are based on ALL the information provided and on knowledge and understanding you have gained whilst studying the course.

1. (a) Describe the benefits to Toyota of maintaining a product portfolio, as shown in **Exhibit 2**.   3

   (b) Justify the methods Toyota uses to ensure quality.   4

   (c) Explain the advantages of Toyota's inventory management system, as identified in the case study.   4

   (d) (i) Describe **3** steps that Toyota may take in its workforce planning.   3

       (ii) Explain the reasons for Toyota's choice of production method.   4

   (e) Explain the impact on Toyota of the external factors listed in the SWOT analysis, as shown in **Exhibit 1**.   5

   (f) Describe possible reasons for Toyota's trends in the following ratios, as shown in **Exhibit 3**:
       • Current Ratio
       • Return on Equity Employed.   4

   (g) Justify, using examples from the case study, the methods Toyota has used to demonstrate Corporate Social Responsibility.   3

[Turn over

MARKS

SECTION 2 — 60 marks
Attempt ALL questions

2. (a) Describe the features of Maslow's motivation theory.   5

    (b) Explain the benefits of positive employee relations.   3

    (c) Describe the impact of current employment legislation on organisations.   4

    (d) Describe the following appraisal methods:
         • one-to-one
         • 360-degree
         • peer-to-peer.   3

3. (a) Discuss the sources of finance available to a public limited company (plc).   4

    (b) Explain the benefits of preparing a cash budget.   5

    (c) Compare the use of functional grouping with product grouping.   4

    (d) Justify the use of spreadsheets in the finance department.   2

4. (a) Describe examples of conflict that may arise between different groups of
         stakeholders.   2

    (b) Discuss the methods of growth that can be used by organisations.   8

    (c) Distinguish between a strategic decision and a tactical decision.   2

    (d) Describe **3** internal constraints that can make decision making difficult.   3

5. (a) Describe the following elements of the extended marketing mix:
         • people
         • process
         • physical evidence.   6

    (b) Discuss the use of centralised warehousing.   3

    (c) Describe the following pricing strategies:
         • skimming
         • penetration
         • discrimination.   6

END OF SPECIMEN QUESTION PAPER

[BLANK PAGE]

DO NOT WRITE ON THIS PAGE

[BLANK PAGE]

DO NOT WRITE ON THIS PAGE

HIGHER

Answers

HIGHER BUSINESS MANAGEMENT
2016

SECTION 1

Question			Expected answer(s)	Max mark
1	a	i	**Premium pricing** • A high price is set • Can give an impression of quality/exclusive image **Competitive pricing** • Price is set similar to competitors • Requires effective promotion/advertising **Market skimming** • Price is initially set high but will lower over time • Customers may want to try the product when it is introduced • High profit margins during the introduction stage help recover costs • Over time the price decreases • Effective for new product launches with few competitors **Penetration pricing** • May be used to launch ice cream into a new market • A low price is initially set • With more sales over time the price will increase **Promotional pricing** • Vouchers/offers/discounts are used to encourage customers to buy • Price may be lowered for a period of time • Used to quickly sell stock and aid cash flow Loss leader… Destroyer pricing… Psychological pricing… Cost-plus pricing…	4
		ii	**Special offers/Save £1/Discount** • Price can be lowered for a period of time • Useful promotion method for shifting stock • Encourages new customers to purchase • Retain loyal customers • Can lower potential profit margin • Customers feel they are getting value for money **Competitions** • Customers have a chance of winning through purchasing a product • May incur additional marketing costs • Can gather marking details from customers, e.g. email, phone number, etc. • Encourages repeat custom to increase the chance of winning	4
	b		• Having different products such as crisps and ice cream spreads the risk therefore reducing the chances of making a loss • Cope with seasonal changes, e.g. ice cream sells well in the summer so can provide higher revenue for this period • All products can be branded, e.g. the crisps and the ice cream produce and therefore enhances the company image • Customers who are loyal may buy multiple products, such as ice cream and chocolate, which will increase sales • Can give a competitive edge to a company encouraging sales over rivals, e.g. selling ice cream suitable for diabetics • The company may be worth more if it were to be sold or parts divested, i.e. selling off crisp production • Can be efficient, e.g. using the same production/employees to make ice cream and ice cubes • Allows for faster growth/easier to expand, e.g. exporting crisps into other countries • Joint venture with Taypack means new skills can be brought in when developing products, e.g. Taypack were potato specialists	4

Question			Expected answer(s)	Max mark

	c		• Provides possibly endless energy
			• Reduces running costs by saving the company £500,000/£280,000 a year
			  • Finance saved can be invested into better machinery
			• Scotland is very windy so there is plenty supply for wind turbine energy
			• Surplus of energy is sold for additional income
			• Helps meet the company's objective — to be the greenest company in Britain
			  • Helps meet the Government objective
			  • Can give the company a good image/reputation
			• Reduces emissions — saved 3,480 tonnes of carbon emissions
			• Customers may be attracted to purchase Mackie's goods as they care about the environment
			  • Provide a competitive edge
				3

	d		• Job production is labour intensive whereas Mackie's production is more capital intensive • Job production is when one product is made at a time whereas flow/batch/mass production is when multiple products are made at a time • Higher prices may be charged for job production as it is a one-off whereas Mackie's production can spread cost over multiple units/can benefit from economies of scale • Job production can customise individual products but Mackie's production can only customise each batch/run • Job production can be more motivating as the product changes/less repetitive... • Both methods of production can be expensive in terms of staff training and machinery	4
	e		**Quality inputs** • Products are carefully sourced from local/reliable suppliers which results in better quality output, e.g. fresher produce (materials) • Staff are trained meaning they are skilled so less likely to make mistakes (labour) • Can be motivating for staff to receive training **Taste panel/Quality circle** • A group of employees who taste the goods to check the quality • May reduce complaints from customers/retailers if produce is checked thoroughly • May empower employees who are involved, increasing motivation **Quality assurance** • Quality checked throughout production • Mistakes are identified quickly reduces waste/saves money • Can be expensive due to the requirement of regular checks **Quality control** • Checks of only inputs and outputs • Cheaper than quality assurance as fewer checks are required **Continuous improvement** • Better machinery can result in better output • Requires a commitment from management **Benchmarking** • Best practice is identified from a competitor/market leader and targets are set • Increases competitiveness • Can be difficult to find a suitable company to benchmark	5
	f	i	**Gross Profit ratio** • Gross Profit/Sales Revenue × 100 **OR** Amount of gross profit made from every £ of sales • Percentage of profit made on sales before expenses are deducted/from buying and selling inventory **Profit For The Year ratio** • Profit For The Year/Sales Revenue × 100 **OR** Amount of net profit made from every £ of sales • Percentage of profit made on sales after expenses are deducted	3

Question			Expected answer(s)	Max mark
		ii	**Gross Profit has <u>decreased</u> possibly due to:**	3
			• Sales revenue has decreased, e.g. sales price has fallen/fewer customers purchasing • Wet summers reduce ice cream sales • Suppliers prices increasing • Economic recession • Competitive market	
			Profit For The Year has <u>decreased</u> in 2012 possibly due to:	
			• Wage costs may have risen • Marketing costs increased • Other income could have decreased	
			Profit For The Year has <u>increased</u> in 2013 possibly due to:	
			• Cheaper supplier • Cheaper/reduced energy • Less borrowing • Reduced wages • More automation • Cheaper advertising methods, e.g. social media	

SECTION 2

Question			Expected answer(s)	Max mark

2	a		• **Bonus/Performance-related pay** — an additional payment on top of a basic wage or salary which will be received when agreed targets are met
			• **Commission** — calculated as a percentage of sales value made by the employee and is added to a basic wage
			• **Piece rate** — when the employee is paid per item they produce
			  • Quality may be compromised if workers are rushing to increase output
			• **Overtime** — paid when an employee works longer than their contractual hours at a higher rate than their basic rate of pay
			• **Share-save schemes** — this is when employees save regular amounts each month for a set period after which their savings can be turned into shares in the business to be kept or sold at a profit
			• **Fringe benefits** — rewards offered to employees as well as their wage/salary, e.g. company car, discount, gym membership, etc.
			  • A company car can make the employee loyal to the firm/retain the worker
			
			Empowerment...
			Job enrichment...
			Promotion prospects...
			Good rate of pay...
			Good working conditions...
			Quality circle...
			Appraisal...
			Work council...
			Worker director...
			Positive corporate culture...
			Open door policy...
			Team working/building...
				4

	b		• Good practice can be acknowledged which motivates the employee • Good practice can be highlighted and shared with all employees within the organisation, which can then be followed by the other employees • Improvements to policies and procedures can be made due to feedback from staff • Training needs can be identified which can increase quality standards • The firm can ensure all employees are aware of the organisation's aims and are working towards achieving these • Strong relationships are formed between manager and employee as they are given the opportunity to have a professional discussion • Targets will be set for the employee which motivates them to be successful by giving them a goal to work towards • Wage increases and bonus can be linked to the appraisal system and administered as they are based on performance which can be viewed as a fairer system • Staff are highlighted for promotion which will retain a core workforce	4

Question			Expected answer(s)	Max mark
	c		• Gaps in the current staffing can be identified • Strategies can be put in place in order to fill gaps in staffing • Relevant training can be given • Staffing forecasts can be carried out • Allows continuity of production • Avoid overstaffing/surplus • Save costs through the use of outsourcing and sub-contracting • Flexible working practices may be considered so that staff are available when they are needed most • Workforce planning encourages managers to prepare and plan for changes rather than simply react to them • Allows businesses to prepare for periods of significant change, e.g. restructuring, technological change, growth, etc.	2
3	a		• No loss of control as the business is not integrating with others • Launch new products/services means businesses can target different markets • Exporting existing products abroad widens their market • Open new physical branches means they can reach new markets by opening up in new locations • Expand existing premises to cater for more products/staff and make more sales • Selling online the business can trade 24/7 around the world • Hire more staff will bring in new ideas to the business to develop new products/increase production, etc. • Increase production capacity by investing in new capital and technology to make more products themselves	4
	b		**Advantages** • Each division can meet the needs of local markets, e.g. different tastes or fashions in different towns or countries • The business can react to changing external (PESTEC) factors quickly • Easy to identify a failing division • Can hold divisional mangers accountable • Can communicate better with the local area, e.g. different languages **Disadvantages** • Duplication of resources, such as administration staff or IT equipment across each division • Divisions may compete against each other • A new division must established if a new area is targeted	3
	c		• Help tackle social problems it has chosen • Some funding/grants/support is only available to social enterprises • Publicity for the social issue promotes the business • Attract customers who appreciate the good causes they help • Attract good quality staff who want to help the social cause • Can make use of an asset lock • Can sell shares to raise finance if they are a limited company	3

4	a	i	• Cannot collude with other organisations to fix prices, e.g. cartel
			  • Cannot fix the bid for tendering on projects with other firms
			• Cannot use market power to pay unfairly low prices to suppliers
			• Prevents monopolies occurring
			  • Block mergers and take-overs that are deemed anti-competitive
			  • Enforcing the selling of divisions/branches/premises, e.g. divestment
			• May be forced change prices
			• May be fined for anti-competitive behaviour
				2

		ii	**Political** • Legislation and regulations will affect an organisation in that they need to comply with the laws **Economic** • Factors such as inflation, recession/boom periods, interest rates will affect organisations in a number of ways, i.e. consumers not spending as much on luxury items/more expensive to borrow money **Social** • Changes in trends and fashions mean that organisations must continually carry out market research **Technological** • As technology changes organisations must keep up-to-date and this will involve a large financial cost **Environmental** • Organisations now attempt to be socially responsible and environmentally friendly to possibly comply with legislation/satisfy consumer groups • Weather/flooding can mean a loss in sales if organisation cannot open due to flooding	5

Question			Expected answer(s)	Max mark
	b		• Tactical decisions are made to achieve the strategic objectives whereas an operational decision is made to ensure smooth running of the business on a daily basis • Tactical decisions are normally made by middle managers whereas operational decisions can be made by any level of management (most likely to be lower level) • Tactical decisions are more likely to be medium term whereas operational are day-to-day • Tactical decisions have a medium level of risk however operational decisions have little or no risk	3

5	a		• Performs "What if" scenarios, e.g. IF statement
			• Produces graphs and charts
			• Formulae calculations are carried out instantly and accurately
			  • Formulae are amended automatically when the spreadsheet is amended
			  • Formulae can be replicated
			• Easy to edit/amend
			• Conditionally format data
			• Can secure data with passwords
			• Can use templates for financial statements
				4

	b		• **Database** — can be used to sort large quantities of information on suppliers and customers
			• **Word Processor** — can be used to send letters and invoices to customers
			  • Preparing financial reports
			• **PowerPoint** — used to present information to staff
			• **Internet** — used to check share prices/exchange rates
			  • **Online banking** saves travelling to the bank
			• **Video-conferencing** — finance manager can hold meetings with other managers without leaving their office
			• **Email** — messages can be sent to more than one employee at a time
			• **Attachments** — can be sent to customers, e.g. invoices
			• **Network (LAN/4G/Cloud)** — can share files with all staff members
			• **Smartphone** — allows for teleworking/remote meetings
			  • **Apps** - allow for portable accounting software, e.g. Sage and Quickbooks
			
			Electronic Point Of Sales (EPOS)...
			Electronic Funds Transfer Points Of Sale (EFTPOS)...
				6

HIGHER BUSINESS MANAGEMENT
2017

SECTION 1

Question			Expected answer(s)	Max mark
1	a		Responses could include the following: • Mary's Meals aims to support a school feeding programme for children all over the world, whereas a public sector organisation aims to provide a service to a local/regional area • Mary's Meals has an objective to maximise donations, whereas a public sector organisation has the objective to use public funds effectively • Both Mary's Meals and a public sector organisation aim to provide the best service possible • Both organisations aim to support education in the community • Both organisations have the objective to be socially responsible • Both organisations aim to support people in poverty Accept any other suitable response	3

	b		Responses could include the following:
			
			• It may be cheaper to import food/materials but this would create more pollution which could result in a poor image for the company
			  • Importing goods would not support local business which could lower respect in the area
			• Legislation differences may exist limiting the activities of Mary's Meals
			  • It can be expensive to train staff in new legislation requirements
			  • Quotas could be imposed limiting business activity
			• Varied taxation and accounting requirements may be imposed between countries which could complicate financial transactions
			• Cultural differences could result in the need to retrain staff or risk offending locals
			• Working hours and conditions may vary which could result in HR issues for transferred staff
			• Language barriers can exist making communication problematic
			
			Accept any other suitable response
				5

	c		Responses could include the following: • **Website** using text and images online to market to a global audience • **Celebrity endorsement** such as Gerard Butler can raise awareness amongst fans • **Animation** such as the Saving Grace story showing moving images and sound to convey information • **Sponsorship** of a school will raise awareness at events in return for support • **Stage work** such as film-making to raise awareness to a large audience Accept any other suitable response	5
	d		Responses could include the following: • Creates a positive image for the organisation which can allow them to attract high quality staff in the recruitment process • May allow them to receive grants and incentives by complying with government policy • More likely to receive donations and therefore increase funds • A good reputation from good word of mouth will raise awareness of the organisation • Help to achieve the company mission statement and objectives Accept any other suitable response	3

Question		Expected answer(s)	Max mark

e		Responses could include the following:
		
		• **Postal surveys** can be sent out to donors' homes and returned
		  • Target an area at a relatively low cost
		  • Low success rate as many people consider postal surveys as junk mail
		• **Face-to-face interviews** provide instant feedback/clarification
		  • Allows for body language/facial expressions to be seen which can improve communication
		  • Can persuade people to donate more effectively if face-to-face
		  • Poor interviewer/personality may intimidate
		• **Customer/employee focus groups** give a range of opinions from a diverse group
		  • May be expensive to run as often members need paid
		• **Telephone surveys** often carried out by calling and asking questions remotely
		  • Often seen as a nuisance and therefore may suffer for a low response rate
		• Online survey…
		• Desk research…
		
		Accept any other suitable response
			6

f	i	Responses could include the following: • Due to an increase in promotional methods used by Mary's Meals • A change of culture as society becomes more responsive to ethical businesses • More disposable income in the economy • An increase in fundraising and charitable events • The website allows for donations to be made online Accept any other suitable response	2
	ii	Responses could include the following: • Donations do not have to be paid back unlike a bank loan which requires the amount to be repaid over time with interest • Donations vary in amount unlike a bank loan which is a specified amount • A bank loan can be requested up front at a far greater amount than donations for expansion purposes • Donations may take longer to receive, whereas a bank loan could be delivered in full if terms are met • Commercial mortgage is taken out against a property, whereas a bank overdraft is short-term access to finance which is expected to be paid off quickly • Venture capital… • Government grant… • Hire purchase/leasing… Accept any other suitable response	2
g		Responses could include the following: • An absence of volunteers/available staff could result in low productivity and fewer children being fed • A lack of donations/funding or appropriate budgeting can result in reduced services • Some volunteers/employees may lack skill which could lead to poor workmanship • Managers may lack experience to launch projects successfully which can damage the organisation's reputation • There may be a lack of information available leading to poor decision making • Poorly maintained technology could break down resulting in a halt in service • Networks and company wifi availability allows its volunteers to stay better informed around the world Accept any other suitable response	4

SECTION 2

Question			Expected answer(s)	Max mark
2	a		Responses could include:	3
			• Through uniforms, staff will form an identity with the organisation which should result in lower staff turnover/absences	
			• Increased staff motivation because they feel part of the organisation/associate strongly with the culture	
			• A single corporate identity is seen by customers which means they will then associate it with that organisation's brands/ethics/logos, etc.	
			• Easily be recognised worldwide meaning customers will feel comfortable with products wherever they are	
			• Values/beliefs/perks can attract quality staff which results in a better quality service	
			• Customer satisfaction can improve because the customers begin to associate with the brands/logos/ethics they like	
			• Can attract new customers as they agree with the aims of the organisation	
			• Customers may become loyal...	
			• Staff can move between branches/departments more easily as they will all be using the same policies and practices	
			• Workspace design/layout...	
			• Open door policy...	
	b		Responses could include:	5
			• Managers are in charge of more staff	
			• Managers can be placed under more stress	
			• Decision making can be slower due to a larger workload	
			• Could result in less managerial promotions	
			• Can mean managers have very little time to spend with each employee to discuss work	
			• Staff could become demotivated	
			• It can be motivational for managers as they have more responsibility	
			• Managers will have less time for planning	
			• May result in poor decisions	
			• Managers can delegate to staff with appropriate skills	
			• Subordinates may resent additional responsibility	
			• Delegation can motivate/empower staff	
	c		Responses could include:	2
			• Employees are likely to want higher wages than the owners/managers are willing to pay	
			• Owners/managers may need to reorganise the business but employees may feel this gives them extra responsibility without training or extra reward	
			• Owners want to maintain control of their business but managers can become too powerful and influential through their decision making	
			• Managers may focus on their objectives for financial reward which will conflict with owner's desire for maximum profit	
			• Customers want delivery of goods as soon as possible but the managers cannot meet customer expectation because of the cost	
			• Managers want to delay payment for goods bought to improve cash flow but suppliers want their money as soon as possible to avoid cash flow issues of their own	

Question			Expected answer(s)	Max mark
3	a		Responses could include:	4
			• Identifies best practice in the market therefore will improve the performance of the organisation if those techniques are adopted • It enhances competitiveness • It is a continuous process of striving to improve • Can be motivational for employees giving them goals to achieve • May identify other functions that could be improved • It can be difficult to gather all the relevant information needed as it is often not publicised • It can be time consuming to study and analyse competitors' techniques • Techniques may not be able to be adopted by the organisation due to internal constraints, e.g. limited finance • Can only be as good as the benchmark set • Minimise the risk of the product failing when launched onto market	
	b		Responses could include:	3
			• Purchase recyclable materials • Reusing waste from the production line • Reduce carbon footprint • Minimise noise pollution created by the manufacturing process • Use sustainable energy, e.g. install solar panels or build a wind farm • Use less packaging of products	
	c		Responses could include:	3
			• Products are unique • Made to suit customers' requirements • Higher prices can be charged • The product can be altered during production process • Seeing a job through can be motivating for employees • Highly skilled workers make quality products	
4	a		Responses could include:	5

			• It shows whether the business will have a surplus of cash which will allow them to plan future purchases
			• It shows whether the business will have a deficit which will allow them to make adjustments to spending
			  • Or arrange an injection of cash to avoid the deficit
			• To make comparisons between predicted and actual figures this will help monitor the performance of the business
			• Highlighting periods where expenses may be high will allow action to be taken to control spending
			• It aids decision making as it provides cash flow information for decisions to be based on
			• It can be used to set targets for individual departments to achieve which will allow the business to stay within budget as predicted
			  • Targets set can also help motivate employees as they have goals to work towards
			• It can empower employees as each department can be set a budget which will give department managers responsibility of spending and recording their finances	

	b		Responses could include:	5
			• Inability to pay suppliers • Raw materials may not be supplied • Unable to pay expenses • May need to find a cheaper supplier • May have to offer discounts to encourage customers on credit to pay early • Increased costs due to borrowing funds, i.e. interest and bank charges • Lack of disposable funds to invest, e.g. to purchase new technology • Low employee morale due to pressure to increase sales revenue • Restricted growth as there is no funds to invest in and support growing the businesses operations • Owner may need to reduce their drawings • May need to sell unused assets • May need to reduce prices of goods • Might lead to staff redundancies • Solvency risk/closure/administration	

Question			Expected answer(s)	Max mark
5	a		Responses could include: • Allows employees to make decisions once they have been given a task • Employees are expected to solve problems on their own with very little guidance from the group leader • Leaders only step in if they are needed/asked • Laissez-faire leadership can be effective in situations where employees are highly skilled, motivated, and capable of working on their own • Inexperienced staff will not be given much direction/support • Could result in poor quality of work • Employees may feel more pressure and become stressed	3

	b		Responses could include:
			
			Equality Act
			• The organisation may be prosecuted for discrimination, e.g. fine
			• Employers may have to revise their recruitment policies
			• Pay both genders the same for jobs of equal value
			• Wording in job adverts must not be discriminatory
			• Invest in better accessibility, e.g. installing lifts, ramps, etc.
			• Investigate issues of discrimination/harassment/victimisation against an employee, customer or a third party
			• Train staff on discrimination prevention/awareness
			
			National Minimum Wage Act
			• An increase in minimum wage leads to increased costs for the organisation
			  • This could result in lowered profits as wage expenses increase
			• If it is found that an organisation has not been paying the minimum wage, they may be required to make a backdated payment for employees
			
			Health and Safety at Work Act
			• Must provide the correct safety equipment
			• Could be temporarily closed or shut down for non-compliance
			• Potential for legal action by members of staff if they suffer injury at work due to non-compliance
			  • This may result in compensation payments
			
			Employment Rights Act
			• Issue employees with payslips
			• Must have a written disciplinary policy in place if over a certain size
			• May be time consuming and costly to implement/update policies and procedures
			• Must issue employees with a contract after a certain period of time
			
			Data Protection Act …
				4

	c		Responses could include:
			
			• Employees may become a registered member of a professional institute
			  • Can increase salary when qualified
			• Employees can be awarded "in-house" certificates once training has been completed
			• Employees may have better chance of promotion after training as training is relevant to the job
			  • However, may leave for a better paid job after gaining qualification
			• Training can be logged in their CPD record to comply with minimum training standards/contracted development time
			• Work-based qualification can be tailored to suit the firm's needs
			• Training normally takes place in the workplace which can save costs for the organisation
			• Can be time consuming as it could be done on a part-time basis
			• Can be costly to pay for the trainers
				3

HIGHER BUSINESS MANAGEMENT
2018

SECTION 1

Question			Expected answer(s)	Max mark

1	a		Responses could include:
			
			• Increased sales revenue/market share/increased profitability.
			• Access to a wider market.
			• Increased brand awareness.
			• Can specialise in different countries.
			• Decreased cost of production.
			    • Lower wage rates.
			• Greater economies of scale.
			• Availability of skilled workers.
			• Access to cheaper suppliers.
			• Take advantage of other countries' Government incentives e.g. tax breaks, grants.
			• Lower rates of corporation tax in different countries.
			• Legislation in other countries may be more relaxed.
			• Avoid barriers to trade/quotas.
			    • Avoid tariffs.
				5

	b		Responses could include: **Horizontal integration/Takeover** • Eliminates one of BT's competitors — so BT can raise prices. • Inherit EE's <u>31 million customers</u> — which will increase BT's market share. • <u>To accelerate its growth</u> — by moving into a new market by purchasing an established firm. • Allows BT to achieve greater economies of scale — which may lower BT's costs. • BT will acquire the assets of EE e.g. premises, networks, transmitters — which are valuable and will contribute to BT's financial position. • As EE was one of the <u>leading mobile network operators</u> — this gives BT a more dominant position in the market. • Which will reduce its risk of failure. • <u>Largest 4G customer base in Europe</u> — which provides a platform to European markets. • <u>Provides innovative and seamless communication services</u> — which will lead to better customer satisfaction.	4

	c		Responses could include:
			
			BT Apprenticeship Scheme
			
			• A professional qualification can be gained.
			• Will gain new/valuable skills specific to the job role.
			• Will gain practical experience and theoretical knowledge.
			• Supported during training.
			    • Will be less costly than outsourcing the training.
			• It involves a high degree of supervision from an experienced member of staff.
			    • It is an expensive method of training.
			    • It is a time consuming method of training.
			• Inexperienced apprentices may make mistakes.
			• No guarantee of a job once the apprenticeship is complete.
			• Apprentices are paid as they train.
			
			BT Academy/Off-the-Job
			
			• Delivered by specialists.
			• Can be tailored to the organisation's needs.
			• Employees can focus on training as they have no workplace distractions.
			• Existing staff aren't hindered or distracted by trainees.
			• Increased productivity when employees return to work after training.
			• Makes BT an attractive employer so will attract the best staff.
			• Decreased productivity whilst training takes place.
			• Travel and accommodation expenses may be incurred.
			• Employee may leave for a better job after the training.
			• May be motivating for staff.
				6

Question			Expected answer(s)	Max mark

	d		Responses could include:
			
			Gross Profit Ratio
			
			• Increasing the selling price of its product.
			• Decrease cost of sales.
			   • Finding a cheaper supplier.
			   • Negotiating trade discounts.
			
			Profit for the Year Ratio
			
			• Increase the gross profit figure.
			• Decrease expenses.
			   • Finding premises with lower rent.
			
			Current Ratio
			
			• Increasing current assets.
			   • Increase sales by offering discounts/advertising etc.
			   • Sell non-current assets.
			• Decreasing current liabilities.
				3

	e		Responses could include: **4K Ultra HD** **Development stage** • Development stage so it is making a loss. • Making a loss as the product is not on sale yet. • Making a loss as the product has incurred costs. **OR** **Introduction stage** • Introduction stage so it is making a loss/profits are low. • Making a loss as sales are low. • Additional expenses/costs are involved. **BT Public Payphones (Decline Stage)** • Decline stage so profits are low/falling. • Sales/demand are in decline therefore profits are falling. • Costs may be higher than income therefore a loss could be made.	2
	f		Responses could include: **Application Forms/CV** • Allows BT to compare candidates like for like as they are asked the same questions. • Can be compared to the person specification to identify if they have the adequate skills and experience for the position. • BT set the questions so can tailor the application form to its own requirements. • Candidate can decide on the CV's content. **Telephone Interview** • Opportunity to hear the applicants' 'phone voice'. • Less time consuming for the candidate as they don't have to travel. • No travel expenses for the organisation. **Attainment Tests** • Can measure the knowledge and skills of a candidate required for the position. • Performance of candidates can be directly compared. **Panel Interview** • In-depth response can be gained from candidates as development of answers can be requested when required. • Can gauge how candidates cope under pressure. • Panel provides a more objective judgement. • Can judge more than just responses e.g. candidate's communication skills, appearance, personality, etc. **Assessment Centres** • Can assess candidates by observing and monitoring their performance in different scenarios e.g. role play, team building etc. • Assessed by specialist staff.	6

Question			Expected answer(s)	Max mark
	g		Responses could include:	4
			Shareholders/Owners and Customer/NHS	
			• Shareholders want high dividends whereas customers want low prices.	
			Shareholders and Employees	
			• Shareholders want high profits whereas employees want high wages.	
			Shareholders and Government	
			• Shareholders want high profits whereas government want all legislation followed which could increase costs.	
			• Shareholders want a low rate of tax whereas the government may wish to increase it.	
			Shareholders and Managers/Chief Executive	
			• Shareholders will be looking for a return on their investment whereas managers may want to reinvest profits for product development.	
			Managers and Suppliers	
			• Managers want to delay payment of suppliers whereas suppliers want prompt payment.	
			Employees and Government	
			• Employees want a low rate of income tax whereas government may wish to increase it.	

SECTION 2

Question			Expected answer(s)	Max mark
2	a		Responses could include:	5
			• Less storage may lower rent/premises costs.	
			• Finance is not tied up in inventory.	
			• So can be better used elsewhere.	
			• Improved cash flow.	
			• Reduced waste as less inventory is stored.	
			• Reduced risk from perishables going 'out of date'.	
			• Reduced risk from fashion changes.	
			• Reduced theft as inventory is easier to monitor.	
			• Dependent on reliable suppliers.	
			• If inventory does not arrive then production will halt.	
			• Increased number of deliveries required e.g. increased administration costs.	
			• May lose out on economies of scale/buying in bulk.	
	b		Responses could include:	3
			• Cheaper for a supplier to deliver to one location.	
			• Bulk purchasing allows for economies of scale/reduced costs/discounts.	
			• Reduces costly duplication of administration/storage facilities.	
			• Items can be found quicker as they are in one place.	
			• Specialist staff may be used.	
			• Improved security.	
			• Theft is reduced.	
			• Standardised procedures can be used.	
			• Accessible if located near infrastructure.	
			• Less space is taken up in departments/outlets.	
	c		Responses could include:	2
			• Identical products can be made.	
			• Can be reprogrammed.	
			• Fewer mistakes/flaws/consistent quality.	
			• Reduces waste.	
			• Less returns/customer complaints.	
			• Reduction in labour costs as fewer employees are needed.	
			• Reduced need for supervision.	
			• Robots do not require a break/holiday/absence/operate 24/7 — **1 max**.	
			• Robots can do work which is repetitive.	
			• Robots can work in conditions employees would not be allowed to for health and safety reasons e.g. in extremely hot conditions.	

Question			Expected answer(s)	Max mark
3	a		Responses could include:	4
			• **Bank loan** which is a sum of money borrowed from a bank and is paid back with interest.	
			• Aids budgeting as it is paid back in instalments.	
			• **Equity** is the issue of shares in return for investment.	
			• **Venture Capital** is investment received in return for a share in the business.	
			• Investments are often given in situation which are seen as too risky by a bank.	
			• **Debenture** is a long-term loan where the holder of the debenture receives annual interest.	
			• The loan must be repaid in full at the end of the agreed period of time.	
			• **Selling off assets** which are no longer needed.	
			• **Sale and lease back** is when the business sells an asset e.g. machinery to raise finance quickly and then rents it back from the company that bought it.	
			• **Mortgage** is a loan given to purchase a property.	
			• Interest is added to the amount borrowed and it is repaid in equal monthly instalments over a long period of time (e.g. 25 years).	
			• **Hire purchase** allows a business to pay for an asset in instalments which is owned after the final payment.	
			• Avoid paying for the asset upfront.	
			• **Leasing** is the renting of an asset.	
			• **Overdraft** allow a business to withdraw cash which it does not have in its account.	
			• **Government grant** does not have to be repaid.	
			Owner's investment is the equity provided by the owner.	
			Retained profits are the profits held within the organisation rather than paying them out to shareholders.	
	b		Responses could include:	4
			• To state the value/net assets of the organisation.	
			• Informs decision making.	
			• Compare with previous years/competitors.	
			• Shows the working equity figure.	
			• Shows the equity of the business/total value of shares.	
			• Used by creditors/suppliers to determine the risk of lending to the organisation/likelihood of repayment.	
			• Used by investors and potential investors to determine the possible return on their investment.	
			• It is a legal requirement.	
			• Can be used to calculate ratios.	
			Shows the value of:	
			• Current assets/trade payables/inventory. — **1 max**	
			• Non-current assets/property/fittings/vehicles. — **1 max**	
			• Current liabilities/trade payables. — **1 max**	
			• Non-current liabilities/long term loans. — **1 max**	
	c		Responses could include:	2
			• Formulae can be entered to carry out calculations.	
			• Minimising human error.	
			• Replication automates calculations.	
			• Charts/graphs can be created.	
			• IF statements can be used to check whether a condition has been met.	
			• Templates can be setup.	
			• Data input may be done by a less-skilled employee.	
			• Can be password protected.	

Question			Expected answer(s)	Max mark
4	a		Responses could include:	5

Focus Groups

- Detailed feedback can be given to the organisation.
- Participants are more likely to give better feedback as they have agreed to take part.
- Qualitative information can be difficult to analyse.

Personal Interviews

- Interviews allow the organisation to directly gain the views of customers.
- Can clarify any questions to aid understanding.
- It can be time consuming to carry out the interview.
- Respondents may lie to get through the interview quickly.

Telephone Survey

- Telephone surveys mean instant feedback can be given.
- Sometimes gains a hostile response from the person being called.

Postal Survey

- Postal survey can be sent out to all customers (wide geographical area).
- Can target customers in selected areas.
- Customers can compete the survey at a time that suits them.
- Low response rate as often viewed as 'junk mail'.
- Cannot ask for clarification.

Hall Test

- Relatively inexpensive to carry out.
- Feedback can be gathered instantly.
- As customer is giving feedback directly, they may not want to give a negative response.

Observation

- Can provide accurate quantitative information.
- Customers will act naturally as they do not know they are getting watched.
- There is no direct contact with customers to ask about their actions.

Test Marketing

- Once feedback is received changes can be made to the product prior to launch.
- Not representative of the wider market as only a small area gets to test the product.

Social Networking Websites

- Can gather large amounts of information quickly.
- Can only gather information from those who use social media.
- Comments are 'public' so anyone can read reviews including competitors.

Internet

- Customers can be surveyed across a wide geographical area.
- Software enables easy analysis of the results.
- Access to the internet must be available.

Consumer audit

- Customer trends can be identified.
- Customers are paid so this can be an expensive method.

EPOS

- Gathers information about consumer behaviour, e.g. what is bought, how they react to changes in price or promotions.
- Promotions can be tailored to the individual customer.
- Expensive to set up.
- If money-off vouchers are offered, it may lower profits.

Newspapers

- Easily accessible as the information already exists.
- May be biased.
- Has been gathered for an alternative purpose.

Question			Expected answer(s)	Max mark
	b		Responses could include: • Building awareness/creating a positive image for an organisation. • Generating press releases. • Organising press conferences/managing bad press. • Organising sponsorship. • Promoting CSR. • Donating to charity.	3
	c		Responses could include: • Brings customers into the shop to buy the products — and then customers may be enticed to buy other full priced items. • Can be used in advertising campaigns to attract customers to come into the organisation — therefore increasing the number of customers. • It can create customer loyalty — as customer may be more likely to stay with the organisation rather than going to its competitors. • Customers may purchase the loss leader priced items in bulk — which can increase sales.	2
5	a		Responses could include: • Support a specific cause. • Provide a service. • To continue operating/survival. • Raise awareness and promote the cause. • Maximise its donations. • Increase the number of volunteers available. • To advance education. • To advance religion. • To better a community. • To operate ethically/be socially responsible. • To make a surplus/profit to reinvest for the cause.	3
	b		Responses could include: • Functional grouping organises staff with similar skills and knowledge together whereas customer grouping structures staff around a targeted type of customer/client/supplier. • Functional grouping caters for the whole organisation whereas each customer group will focus on its customers' needs. • It is easier to compare performance for each customer grouping whereas function grouping will show results for the entire organisation. • Functional grouping may be cheaper than customer grouping as there is less duplication. • Customer groups are more responsive to changing customer needs whereas functional groups can lose sight of market changes/may be slow to react. • Both groups can compete with each other inside the organisation. • Both groups allow staff to build expertise/specialise.	4

	c		• **Weather**, such as heavy snowfall, can result in suppliers not being able to deliver goods on time.
			  • Can delay production/sales.
			• **Climate change** may lead to changes in demand for products e.g. warmer coats, therefore, the firm may need to change the products they offer.
			• **Seasonal changes** can lead to changes in customer demand/shopping habits.
			• **A natural disaster** could force the company to close for a period of time which means sales/profits are reduced.
			• **Bio-fuels** will reduce a firm's carbon footprint which will improve its image.
			  • However eco-friendly chemicals are significantly more expensive.
			• **Reducing packaging** can result in the company reducing costs.
			• **Pressure to recycle rubbish/waste** increases the company costs.
			• **Reducing emissions** and waste can increase costs e.g. processing waste, using specialist removal services.
			• **Waste regulations** require businesses to separate metal, plastic, glass, paper and card for collection which takes more time.
			• **Eco taxes** is a tax is placed on activities which are harmful to the environment which results in additional costs for the business.
			• **Renewable energy** — changing to renewable energy such as solar power requires further investment which may result in a business having to borrow to fund it.
			• **Sustainable sourcing** — sourcing products ensures raw materials are not being depleted which means organisations can continue to source these materials in the future.
				3

HIGHER BUSINESS MANAGEMENT
2018 SPECIMEN QUESTION PAPER

Question			Expected response	Max mark
1	a		Responses could include: • risk is spread over different markets • increased profits from selling different models • newer models can replace those at the end of the product life cycle • a range of products increases brand awareness • able to meet the needs of different market segments.	3
	b		Responses could include: **Quality circles/suggestion system** • using members of production staff to suggest improvements • increases staff motivation • workers doing the job often have a better idea than management of how to improve • workers have suggested the ideas themselves so it reduces staff resistance to change. **Quality management** • strong focus on customer, leads to greater customer satisfaction • commitment from all staff, should ensure a high-quality product • quality checked at all stages, means fewer products not being up to standard • highly skilled/trained staff, results in good customer service • quality inputs, leads to a high-quality product or service • zero error tolerance, results in less wastage • high-quality products, lead to loyal customers • high-quality products, result in the organisation having a good reputation • continual improvement, means the organisation stays ahead of the competition.	4

	c		Responses could include:
			
			• supplies are ordered only when they are needed for production — which means there is no wastage of inventory
			• no money is tied up in inventory — which improves cash flow
			• no large warehouse is required — saving on related costs, for example rent/security
			• strong relationships are formed with suppliers — which makes suppliers more responsive to changing external factors/demand
			  • because inventory can be ordered in, at the exact moment trends are identified
			  • therefore inventory is not surplus to requirement if trends in car purchases change
			• there is less chance of theft by staff or customers — because it is easier to supervise minimal inventory.
				4

	d	i	Responses could include: • identify how many workers are needed in a capital-intensive process • analyse the skills required • analyse the current and future staff profile • identify gaps and then close them • identify current staff training needs to meet required skills • train existing staff • recruit and select new staff.	3
		ii	Responses could include: • the type of production will need to be standardised — so a capital-intensive process is more effective • large amounts of cars are required — so capital-intensive production can produce them more quickly • robots can be used 24/7 • if the task is complicated — capital-intensive production allows it to be carried out accurately • robots can perform repetitive work — that a labour force would find boring • robots can carry out dangerous tasks — which reduces accidents • using machines reduces labour — which reduces costs.	4

Question			Expected response	Max mark

	e		Responses could include:
			
			• *changing customer attitudes to 'green' cars* — may give Toyota a competitive edge over other car manufacturers
			• *falling fuel prices* — will mean more customers will be able to afford to buy a car
			• *global economic recovery* — will increase sales because of falling unemployment/higher disposable incomes
			• *competition* — will mean Toyota will have to develop better products
			   • deploy a successful marketing strategy to beat the competition
			• *fluctuating exchange rates* — which may change import/export levels
			• *rising raw material prices* — will increase the production costs
			   • which may reduce profits as expenses will increase
			   • could be passed on to customers by increasing prices
			• *natural disasters, for example earthquakes/tsunamis* — could destroy factories/cause production to cease.
				5

	f		Responses could include: **Current Ratio** • increase in current liabilities • decrease in current assets **Return on Equity Employed** • a decreased gross profit figure • the knock-on effect of this could decrease Profit for the Year • increased expenses • sold additional shares.	4
	g		Responses could include: **Production of an eco-friendly car in order to reduce carbon footprint** • to attract a new market • to improve reputation **Developing fuel efficiency** • can be used as a marketing tool to attract customers looking to reduce fuel costs **Car safety features** • to gain quality and safety awards • can be used as a marketing tool • to compete with other car manufacturers **Toyota academy/quality circles/suggestion system** • to attract new staff • to motivate existing staff • to reduce resistance to change • to improve employee relations.	3

2	a		Responses could include:
			
			• Maslow's theory classifies human needs and how they are related to each other (hierarchy)
			• a person starts at the bottom of the hierarchy and will initially seek to satisfy each stage in order
			• once these needs have been satisfied they are no longer a motivator
			• if management can identify which level each employee has reached they can decide on suitable rewards
			• **physiological (basic) needs** which are, for example, food/shelter
			   • can be satisfied through basic pay
			• **safety needs** which are job security/safe working environment
			   • can be satisfied through permanent contracts
			• **social (love and belonging) needs** where most people want to belong to a group
			   • can be satisfied by working with colleagues who provide support/teamwork/communication
			• **esteem needs** are about being given recognition for a job well done
			   • a promotion might achieve this
			• self-actualisation is when people realise their potential
			   • may be measured by the extent of success and/or challenge at work.
				5

Question		Expected response	Max mark
	b	Responses could include: • employees will have their chance to discuss changes or grievances so they will feel happier and more secure in the workplace • employees will become flexible with suggestions from management making it easier to introduce change within the organisation • disputes will be less likely to arise as employees will have been consulted • employees understand what it is that the employer is trying to achieve • the workforce will be committed, helping to ensure the business meets its objectives • the organisation will gain a good image for treating its employees correctly/maintaining good employee relations, attracting new employees easily.	3

	c	Responses could include:
		
		National Minimum Wage Regulations or National Living Wage Regulations
		• an increase in minimum wage leads to increased costs for the organisation
		   • this could result in lowered profits as wage expenses increase
		• if an organisation has been found to be paying less than the minimum wage, it may be required to make a backdated payment to its employees
		
		Health and Safety at Work Act
		• the organisation must provide the correct safety equipment
		   • increasing costs for safety equipment/training
		• the organisation could be temporarily closed or shut down for non-compliance
		• potential for legal action by members of staff if they suffer injury at work due to non-compliance
		   • this may result in compensation payments
		
		Equality Act
		• it may be prosecuted for discrimination, for example, fined
		• it may have to revise its recruitment policies
		• it must pay both genders the same for jobs of equal value
		• it must not use discriminatory wording in its job adverts
		• it may need to invest in better accessibility, for example installing lifts and ramps
		• it must investigate issues of discrimination/harassment/victimisation against an employee, customer or a third party
		• it must train employees on discrimination prevention/awareness.
			4

	d	Responses could include: **One-to-one** • a regular review of an employee's job performance which is documented and evaluated • review and discussion of last year's targets takes place • targets may be set about future performance • training needs are identified **360-degree** • a review of an employee's job performance, with feedback coming from subordinates, peers, supervisors and the employee themselves • all those involved answer the same questions (often anonymously), which allows for comparison • allows for a variety of viewpoints from colleagues • self-evaluation is an important part of this type of appraisal **Peer-to-peer** • colleagues in the same or similar position are asked to provide feedback on specific aspects of an employee's performance • managers are excluded from this type of appraisal.	3

Question			Expected response	Max mark
3	a		Responses could include: **Share issue** • shareholders become owners of a plc, which may mean founders lose control • large sums of finance can be raised by this method • profits will need to be shared among more shareholders **Government grant** • may take a long time to secure the grant • must meet specific conditions to secure the grant • does not have to be paid back **Bank loan** • repaid in instalments, which aids budgeting • once agreed, a loan is received promptly • interest charges may affect cash flow in a negative way **Commercial mortgage** • repaid with interest over a long term **Debentures** • only interest is paid during the debenture period, while capital is repaid at the end of the period • repayment at the end of the debenture period may affect cash flow • interest needs to be paid, regardless of annual profit • the interest charged is listed as an expense **Venture capital/business angels** • will provide capital when banks think it is too risky • may give advice and support to help improve and/or grow the business **Leasing** • this is renting an asset — at the end of the lease agreement, the leaseholder can receive an updated asse • the leaseholder is responsible for servicing and maintenance of the asset • monthly payments can aid budgeting • if the organisation wants to buy the asset at the end of the lease agreement, it can make a balloon payment • the overall cost of the asset will be higher than purchasing it outright **Sale of assets** • any unnecessary assets can be sold to raise cash and then leased back, if required **Hire purchase** • the cost of buying assets can be spread over a period of time • fixed instalments can aid budgeting • the overall cost of the asset is increased by the interest payments • the asset is not owned by the organisation until the final payment is made **Overdraft** • allows flexibility, as the organisation can spend more than it has in its account • can be pre-arranged if a cash shortfall is expected • attracts high interest charges **Trade credit** • it does not need to pay for goods/raw materials until after they have been received, for example, 30 days later • it may be able to sell goods on, before it has paid for them • customers may also expect to receive trade credit **Debt factoring** • allows an organisation to 'sell' debt on, at lower than its face value/the debt is discounted, so the organisation does not receive the full value of the outstanding debt • it does not need to 'chase up' debt itself • reduces the likelihood of cash flow problems caused by unpaid debts.	4

Question			Expected response	Max mark
	b		Responses could include: • it helps to highlight periods when cash flow problems may occur – which allows the organisation to take corrective action • can be shown to a potential lender – which can then be used to secure borrowing • can be shown to potential investor – who can then see if it is a viable business • it can be used to make comparisons between actual spending and targeted spending – which helps to control costs • it can show periods of surplus cash – which can then be used for capital investment • it can be used to set departments/managers a budget – which gives them a target to focus on • it can be used to aid future financial planning – which can help identify when an overdraft is required.	5
	c		_see table below_	4
	d		Responses could include: • performs 'What if' scenarios/creates IF statements • produces graphs and charts • formulae calculations are carried out instantly and accurately • formulae are amended automatically, when the spreadsheet is amended • formulae can be replicated • editing/amending is simplified • conditionally format data • can secure data with passwords • can use templates for financial statements.	2
4	a		Responses could include: • employees are likely to want higher wages than the owners/managers are willing to pay • managers want to delay payment for goods bought to improve cash flow, but suppliers want their money as soon as possible • customers want delivery of goods as soon as possible, but the managers cannot meet customer expectations • owners/managers may need to reorganise the business, but employees may feel this gives them extra responsibility without training or extra reward • owners want to maintain control of their business, but managers can become too powerful and influential through their decision making • managers may focus on their objectives for financial reward, which may conflict with owners' desire for maximum profit.	2

Question c table:

Functional	whereas	Product
staff with similar expertise work together		staff are organised around a product or service
functional areas work for the benefit of the whole organisation		different divisions work for the benefit of the division
functional areas may compete against each other		different product divisions may compete against each other
performance is measured for the organisation as a whole		it is easier to identify products that are performing poorly
organisation may become large and unresponsive to change		each division is more responsive to customer needs

Question		Expected response	Max mark
	b	Responses could include: **Organic/internal growth:** • open new outlets • operate in more markets and/or countries • introduce new products • less risky than a takeover • can be financed internally • may be limited by the size of the market **External growth/takeover/merger through:** **Backward vertical** • when the business takes over its supplier/source of goods and materials • this guarantees the quality and quantity of inputs • it may limit supplies to competitors • cuts out the middleman/adds to profits **Forward vertical** • when the business takes over a customer • this guarantees an outlet for its products • cuts out the middleman/adds to profits **Horizontal integration** • when two businesses at the same stage in the production process join together • may remove a competitor • the business may dominate the market **Diversification/conglomeration** • where a business moves into an entirely different market • spreads risk • new customers may be attracted to the original product **Lateral** • where two firms merge which are in a related industry but are not in direct competition (for example, a hairdresser and a beauty therapist).	8
	c		2

Strategic	whereas	Tactical
long-term decision		medium-term decision
set out the objectives		taken to achieve objectives
made by senior management		made by middle management
high risk		medium risk

Question		Expected response	Max mark
	d	Responses could include: • the quality and quantity of information available to the manager • the amount of training/experience the manager has had in decision making • the ability and skill of the manager to make decisions • the level of risk the manager is willing to take • lack of finance to carry out the decision • the time available to make the decision • how willing the staff are to cooperate with the decision • lack of equipment/technology to implement the decision • existing company policy may restrict which decisions a manager is allowed to make • a senior management veto of what the manager decides.	3

Question			Expected response	Max mark
5	a		Responses could include: **People** • any member of staff who comes into contact with the customer • the organisation needs to create a culture of good customer care • the organisation may need to create customer service policies • staff are trained in customer care • motivated staff are required • good after-sales service and advice should be available **Process** • the systems and procedures that deliver a product or service • the experience the customer has when making a purchase • the impression left on the customer • the organisation must be able to handle complaints • contingency planning could be put in place • short waiting times • user-friendly internet experience • quality of information given to customers **Physical evidence** • the physical environment experienced by the customer • the layout and design of the premises • the ambience of the premises • the cleanliness of the premises • must reflect customer expectations.	6
	b		**Advantages** • get a bulk buying discount • reduced risk of pilferage • inventory is maintained in appropriate conditions • no space is taken up in departments with storage • specialist staff handle inventory more efficiently • centralised warehousing can be cheaper than using multiple warehouses • centralised warehousing ensures consistent inventory handling procedures • can monitor inventory usage in different departments/sites **Disadvantages** • more time is taken to physically move the inventory from the central warehouse to each department • more admin staff required to deal with the paperwork involved • additional staff increases costs • cost of specialist equipment and storage facilities • may not be reflective of actual inventory usage in each division/branch.	3

	c		Responses should include:
			
			Skimming
			• price is set high initially, when no/little competition exists
			  • appeals to market segments who are keen to own the newest products
			  • allows the business to make high profit
			• when competitors enter the market, the price is lowered
			
			Penetration
			• price is set lower than competitors, to attract customers
			  • used to encourage customers to switch brands
			• once customers start buying the product, the price is raised
			
			Discrimination
			• when a business charges different customers different prices for the same product
			• when a business charges different prices at different times/days for the same product
			  • may be used to sell surplus capacity (eg airline/theatre tickets).
				6

Acknowledgements

Permission has been sought from all relevant copyright holders and Hodder Gibson is grateful for the use of the following:

Extracts and images reproduced by permission of Mackie's of Scotland (2016 pages 2–5);
Image supplied courtesy of 'The Scottish Farmer' © Newsquest (Herald & Times) Ltd. (2016 page 4);
Statistics from Companies House (https://beta.companieshouse.gov.uk/company/SC030096/filing-history).
Contains public sector information licensed under the Open Government Licence v3.0
(https://www.nationalarchives.gov.uk/doc/open-government-licence/version/3/) (2016 page 6);
Logo and extracts taken from http://www.marysmeals.org.uk. Reproduced by permission of Mary's Meals
(2017 pages 2–5);
The information about BT Group plc ("BT"), contained in the exam question on pages 2-4 of the 2018 exam paper, is based on historic information made available by BT and may no longer be accurate. For current information about BT, please visit www.btplc.com.
A case study reproduced by permission of BT Group plc is adapted from The BT Story, BT plc Press Release
25 March 2015 & 2014 BT Group Annual Report, 2017 BT Group Annual Report; and also from BT plc Careers,
MBA Programme, Application Process. Reproduced with permission of BT Group plc (2018 pages 2–4);
Image © 360b/Shutterstock.com (2018 page 2);
A case study reproduced by permission of Toyota (GB) PLC (https://www.toyota.co.uk/) (2018 SQP pages 2–4);
Image © Mrs_ya/Shutterstock.com (2018 SQP page 2);
Image © Steve Lagreca/Shutterstock.com (2018 SQP page 3);
Image © Ed Aldridge/Shutterstock.com (2018 SQP page 4);
Image © Art Konovalov/Shutterstock.com (2018 SQP page 4);
Image © Dong liu/Shutterstock.com (2018 SQP page 4).